Get lost

To three amazing
Cumbrians

Love you ♡

THE LAKE DISTRICT SURVIVAL GUIDE

THE ESSENTIAL TOOLKIT FOR SURVIVING LIFE IN CUMBRIA AS A TOURIST OR LOCAL

IAN YOUNG

CONTENTS

BEFORE YOU START...

To get the best out of your time in the Lake District it's important to stay alive.

If you read this Guide thoroughly and take in all the important points then you might just make it.

You see, the Lake District is a scary place if you don't know what you're doing.

There are mountains.

There are sheep.

And there are Cumbrians.

You might run into poets or middle-aged people wearing lycra.

You may even encounter men rolling around fields in their undies.

If you don't watch out, this might happen:

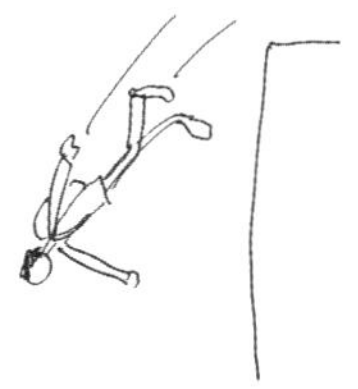

Or this:

200 metres into any walk with an upward incline greater than down your kids will definitely do this:

And I wouldn't mention zip-wires in any pub within 1,000 miles of Thirlmere unless you like the feel of a pitch fork embedded in your chest.

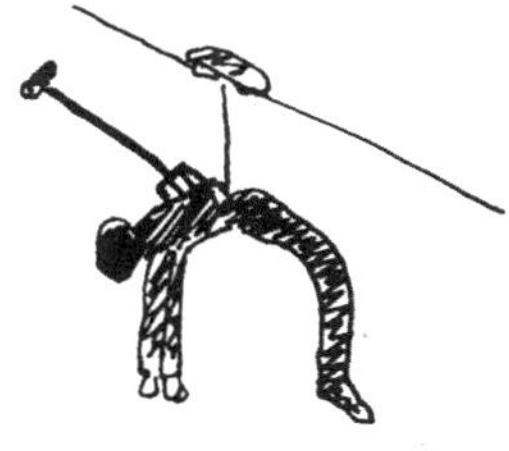

Like the French, the Cumbrians like you to *meyak a la'al effort with t' craic wherivver yer byuts tek yer roond cyownty.*

See how I skilfully dropped into the local dialect there without you noticing.

With a bit of practice you'll get the hang of it.

What I'm trying to say is *you need to be careful.* And the aim of this book is to guide you through the peat hags of uncertainty that could lead to disaster.

To do that, we have advice from the very best. Here's AW – Alfred Wainwright, the original fellwanderer himself. (We'll be hearing more from him throughout the book.)

He's not the friendliest.

Okay, over to Sarah Nelson, world famous gingerbread maker from Grasmere. She'll cheer you up.

...Maybe not.

Let's get started. Firstly, if you're coming to the Lakes you need to know a little bit about Wainwright, just so you don't embarrass yourself in the Dog & Gun while boring people about your epic expedition to Friar's Crag...

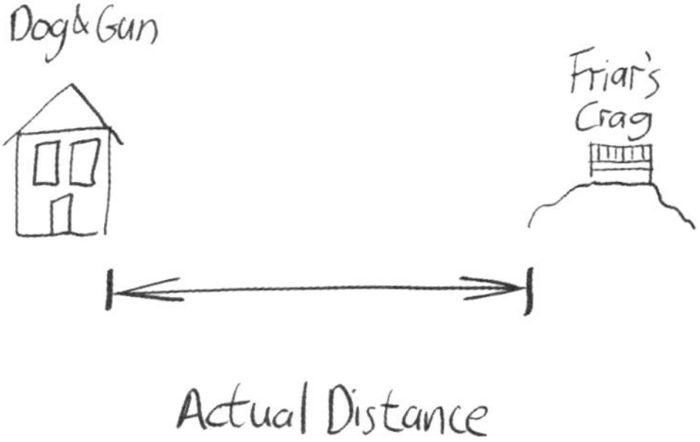

ESSENTIAL KNOWLEDGE

ALFRED WAINWRIGHT

Alfred Wainwright was born in Blackburn in 1907.

His father was an alcoholic and mostly studied gutters close up.

This wasn't great for his career, so the family had no money.

Young Alfred was heading for a life oiling gears and tying yarn at the local mill when he made a good decision; he stayed at school (are you listening kids?).

When he left school he got a job at the town hall and studied accountancy in his spare time.

Life was good for Alfred.

Then he got married.

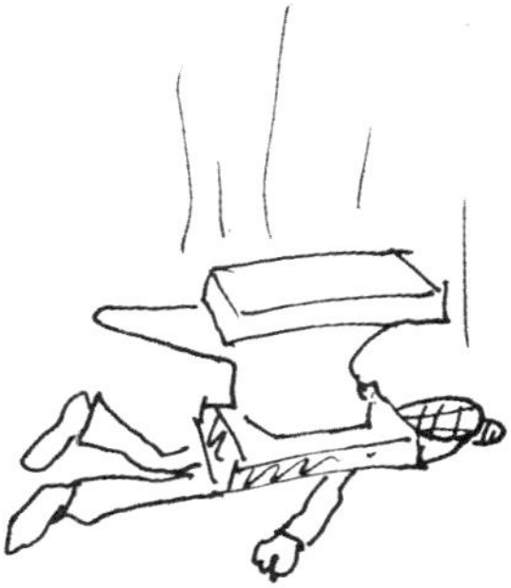

On his wedding night, possibly excited by the impending nuptials, Alfred threw caution to the wind and removed his cap.

This was the first time he'd done so in front of his new bride, Ruth.

It didn't go well.

Wainwright was, she realised, *ginger*.

Ruth was horrified.

Now, I'm not speaking from personal experience here (although my wife may disagree), but being horrified on your wedding night is not the best start to a contented, lifelong commitment.

Decades of marriage lay ahead of him and she hated him from day one*.

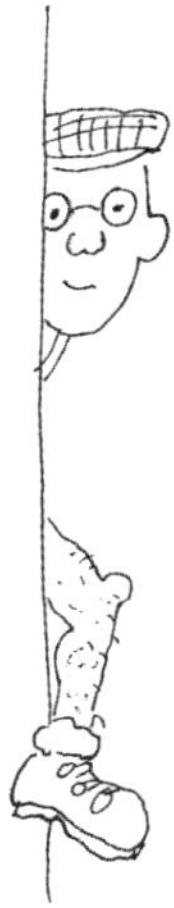

(*Although Alfred must have left his hat on every now and again because they managed to have a son, Peter.)

Apart from the 'Peter night', three-and-a-bit decades of loveless marriage ensued.

To escape the frostiness at home Alfred did the honourable thing and fled for the hills, wandering the Lakeland fells from his new Kendal home in a tweed suit, ignoring his wife and child and pretty much everyone else.

In 1952 he started work on his first *Pictorial Guide*. Here he is hard at work in his study. Sort of overfilled the pipe a little.

If Ruth hadn't been disgusted by the sight of him maybe Alfred would never have started his guides and the Lake District would be a poorer place because of that.

So, thanks Ruth.

ESSENTIAL KNOWLEDGE

THE '214' WAINWRIGHTS

Wainwright referred to his *Guides* as his love letters to the fells, and the 214 fells included in the books are now ingeniously called 'The Wainwrights'.

If you are to survive the Lake District then you need to learn a few of the fell names and drop them into conversations as much as possible.

The locals will still despise you, but at least they'll let you buy them a pint. The more fell names you come up with, the more pints they'll let you buy.

If you meet someone who has done all The Wainwrights, please approach with caution...

If you're too tight-fisted to buy Wainwright's books here's some help fell name-dropping:

Cawfell Dyke
Highest mountain in England

Dog Bells
Popular route near Keswick

Skiddaw Little Big Man
Skiddaw with a chip on its shoulder.

Great Cockup
That's a joke one.

CULTURAL CORNER #1

ART IN THE LAKES

The Lakes aren't all about slogging up mountains until your patellas grind into your tibias. We're a cultured bunch up here. Here's Melvyn, the Braggster, Lord of all Wigton, to tell you about it:

"Art and the Lakes are symbiotic; I'll even go as far as ubiquitary, not that I'd expect you to understand what that means."

Big words turned Lord Bragg into a Southerner, so be careful using them.

Over to you Melvyn:

"Here I am standing on the shores of Coniston. Look down the road and you will see an astonishing piece of art coming towards me. Straight from the streets of New York we have a famous Banksy, 'Sirens of the Lambs', an horrific but also abnormally amusing commentary on the ineffectuality and anguish that.............."

ESSENTIAL KNOWLEDGE

SURVIVING THE LAKE DISTRICT WITH CHILDREN

Getting your kids to walk for more than an hour is one of the most difficult challenges you will ever face.

Second only to getting your two-year-old's back to bend into a car seat outside Tesco.

The problem we have here in the Lakes is the scarcity of flatness.

Last week near Caldbeck I took my daughter and the dog for a tiny little walk.

After 30 minutes of relatively flat walking my daughter suddenly fell to the ground, on her knees, and reached desperately up to the sky.

"Get up for goodness sake." That was me.

"What are we doing, what are we doing out here?" That was her.

This happens every now and again when I've forgotten The Rules.

As my daughter dramatically demonstrated, when walking *kids need a point* – there has to be something in it for them.

How selfish is that?

If you want to have a trouble-free walk, I have found over the years that you need to be prepared.

These are the main ingredients for a successful walk with children:

Haribos: Deep inside your ruck-sack, far from clutching hands, you need the promise of something great. Use this promise with the following sentence: "Just round the next bend we'll stop and have some Haribos."

When the next bend arrives, use the same sentence again without breaking your stride or getting anything out of your rucksack. Replace 'bend' with 'rock', 'bridge' or 'tree' to keep things interesting.

Eventually the promises stop working and you get this again:

Then you can feed them some Haribos.

→ **Caves:** There is nothing more exciting than walking to a cave, as long as you make it sound dangerous. Dragons are good for under-fives, bears for under-10s, and for teenagers: “That roof doesn’t look safe,” followed by: “Are you listening to me? Give me that phone.”

→ **Tree trunks:** Every time you see a fallen tree (that looks safe*) get on there and shout: “Bet you can’t walk all the way to the end without falling off.” If they get close to achieving the task push them off and start them again.

(*If you're a Health and Safety expert this is how I dress my children.

If you're not, no I don't.) →

→ **Stove:** Take a stove and some pasta out with you and do some cooking. Your kids will eat anything when out in the fresh air. Test this theory out with a Brussels sprout and liver stew.

→ **Sticks:** Kids love to look for a really good walking stick, every time they go out. This puts a bit of time in. We have a garden full of old sticks because to leave them would be 'stick cruelty'.

→ **Maps:** This is risky this one, but give your child the map, tell them the route and let them lead the way. They love doing that. When you get lost, running after them will keep them amused for a little longer.

*...if you can't find the car again.

→ **Rivers:** Kids love rivers. Boots off and a bit of paddling works wonders. A tiny bit of ghyll scrambling never fails. I have played 'Pooh Sticks' a zillion times, maybe more, but kids never get tired of it.

TIP: Check for villages upstream before you start.

In an ideal future my children will love the outdoor life as much as I do and we will all go on long, happy hikes together in the warm summer months.

MYTHICAL BEASTS

TIZZIE-WHIZIE

One major hazard you will come across in the Lake District is the plethora of mythical creatures that inhabit the area.

If you like your mythical creatures to come with irrefutable photographic evidence like Nessie then look no further than our own home-grown version: Tizzie-Whizie.

Tizzie-Whizie was first spotted on Windermere by a Bowness boatman around AD1900.

The boatman came to shore and told all the tourists about this amazing creature that could fly across the surface of the lake.

Like all mythical creatures Tizzie-Whizie was shy.

The best way to track it down was to listen for it. To do this the boatman would kindly take you onto the lake (perhaps charging a fee) and make you lean out of the boat with your ear close to the water.

The cry was very faint so you had to lean really close to the surface of the lake, almost touching it, to hear anything. It was amazing how many people mysteriously fell in doing this.

But Tizzie-Whizie was nowhere to be seen.

I have a theory to explain a lot of the mysterious fall-ins, and have drawn a little sketch to explain it:

But, guess what, as usual I'm wrong. The boatman wasn't just booting people in the water for a laugh while making a bit of extra cash.

You know why?

Because the boatman *captured* Tizzie-Whizie. Not only that, but he managed to transport the creature – still alive – to Louis Herbert's Photographic Studio in Bowness.

They calmed Tizzie down with warm milk and biscuits, and managed to get it to sit on a stand long enough to set up a camera.

Then they took a photo, with Tizzie on it, as clear as day.

They were so excited they'd managed to get the photo that they didn't notice Tizzie flying out of an open window. Now I'm not one to judge but, for God's sake, *which idiot left the window open?* Anyway, that doesn't matter. The important thing was they had proof.

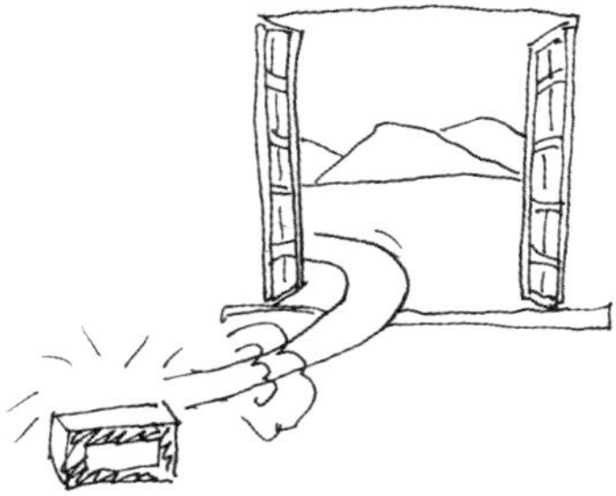

Tizzie-Whizie was real and – prepare yourself in whatever way you can – here's the evidence:

That's right, Tizzie-Whizie is a hedgehog with bee's wings and a squirrel's tail.

Unbelievable you might think, but there's the evidence right in front of you.

The photo was made into a postcard and thousands of them were sold.

There was also a £5 reward for its capture.

But Tizzie-Whizie was never caught again.

Now I've spent a lot of time around Windermere, swimming and walking, but I've never been lucky enough to spot Tizzie whizzing along the lake.

I'm told there are still a lot of sightings.

So make sure you go and have a look, hire a boat and say you heard it from me so I can get my percentage of the Tizzie-Whizie wealth.

LAKELAND STEREOTYPES #1

'THE STRAVA'

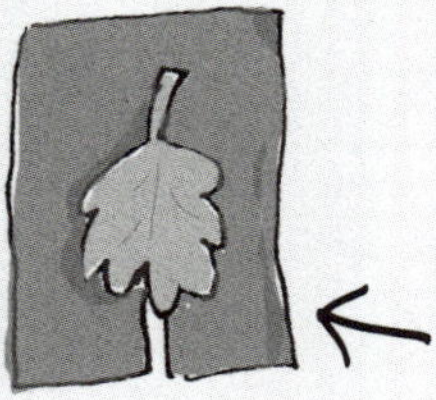

Spend enough time outside in the Lake District and you will see a Strava.

In fact you'll see a lot more of a Strava than you want to, thanks to the snuggly powers of Lycra.

The Strava can't do anything without their stats being recorded and uploaded.

If it's not logged it hasn't been done. They are the rules.

Little do they know that no one else gives a monkey's.

Here's a conversation between a Strava and a normal human being:

GPS

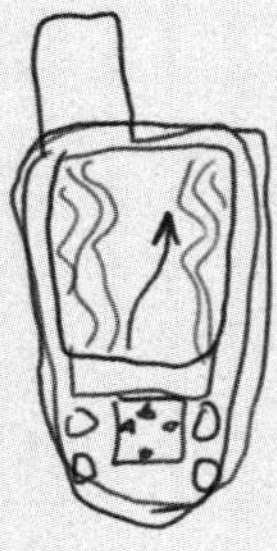

"The good lady wife bought me this fancy new gizmo.

Said I had to carry it with me on my walks.

It knows where I am and it's supposed to tell me where to go.

I'll certainly be telling it where to go if it thinks it can Crinkle Craggin' tell me what to do.

I've spent most of my life trying to get away from her, now she wants to track me?

I just need my own space.

Preferably 912 square miles of it."

LAKELAND FOLK

A POET'S VIEW

It takes a poet; in fact it takes – in his own words – the greatest and most devastatingly handsome of all the Lakeland poets, Samuel Taylor Coleridge, to unambiguously express the treachery of the Lakes.

Hold onto your pituitary gland... Here he goes...

"Ullswater, oh Ullswater, with its thrice-five miles of fertile ground and gardens bright with sinuous rills.

"But oh! Aira Force, that deep romantic chasm, a savage place, beware the ceaseless turmoil, the huge fragments rebounding like hail."

Crikey, it does sound dangerous.

"Stop interrupting, normal person. For you cannot see Borrowdale like I do, where blossoms many an incense-bearing tree. And Derwent, through wood and dale the sacred river ran, sinking in tumult to a lifeless ocean near the steelworks in Workington, where women wail for their demon-lovers.

"And the Buttermere maid, on her dulcimer she played. Singing of Wainwright. Beware! Beware! His flashing eyes, his greying hair! Weave some tweed around him thrice. For he on Kendal Mint Cake has fed and drunk the milk of Skye Farm Dairy."

Okay, that's enough. Just because you nearly fell off Broad Stand on Scafell doesn't make you an expert.

"How dare you, the sight of the Crag! The impetuous clouds just over them, posting so luridly and so rapidly northward, overawed me..."

Yes, yes, let's carry on.

ESSENTIAL KNOWLEDGE

WALKING TECHNIQUES

Here's an exhaustive guide of walking techniques to tackle the Lakeland fells. Read it carefully – it could save your life.

General purpose stance for admiring Borrowdale from Cat Bells.

Useful for speeding up a slow walker.

When the ridge is scary but you don't want to crawl like a baby.

Useful for slowing down a fell runner.

I'm knackered but there's people ahead, so hold form.

Useful for streams in spate and for boulders you can't be bothered walking round.

MUNGRISDALE COMMON

ESSENTIAL KNOWLEDGE

LAKELAND SHEEP

Identifying sheep will definitely impress the farming community. So here's a quick guide:

Herdwick: As you can see the Herdwick looks like Mr Tumnus from Narnia. They have white faces and are very smiley. The ewes don't have horns and they're the ones you're most likely to see on the fells.

Swaledale: Think Princess Leia if she wanted to rob some fags from the local garage. Swaledales have white noses and white around the eyes. The rest of their face is black, which makes them look like robbers. Curly horns are found on both males and females.

Rough Fell: This looks like the love-child of Princess Leia and Don Diego de la Vega who has run very quickly into a dry-stone wall. It has a broader face than the Swaledale, and the Mask of Zorro is a giveaway – although no-one knows its true identity.

→ **Texel:** Half sheep, half Phil Mitchell, this thing looks tough and it's got muscles.

I saw one of these head-butt another sheep in the side once. The head-butted sheep looked shocked and did a 'There's-nothing-I–can-do-about-this-silly-sideways-fall' fall.

Don't mess with The Tex.

It will also do you well to know a few sheep-related farming terms to throw into conversations you might have:

- **Ewe** – Not me.
- **Gimmer** – *Gimmer, gimmer a sheep after midnight.*
- **Tup** – Uncastrated male sheep.
- **Whether** – Opposite of the above. It hurts to think about.
- **Tupping** – Sheep naughtiness.

ESSENTIAL KNOWLEDGE

MEN IN UNDIES

There is nothing more spectacular than seeing two grown men with their undies outside their trousers flying through the air.

In the Lakes it doesn't look quite like that. More like this:

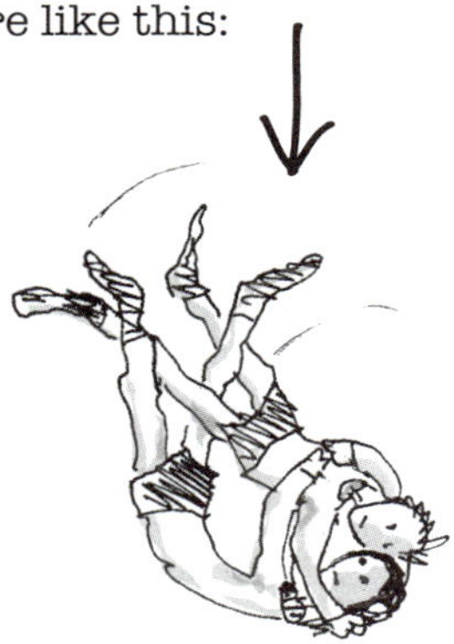

This is Cumberland and Westmorland Wrestling at the Grasmere Show.

If you want to survive the Grasmere Show, one, don't wrestle, and two, don't take the mick out of the costume. It's sensitive.

The costume – or, more accurately, *the strip*, as it's not panto – comprises long johns, embroidered vest and a velvet centrepiece.

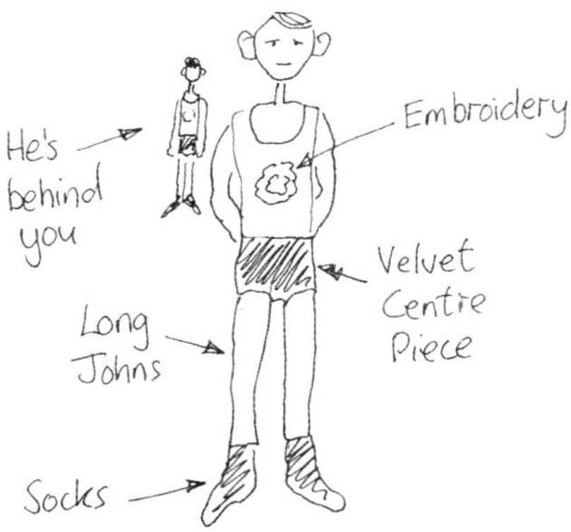

Here's the issue. One newspaper reporter recently called the velvet centrepiece a pair of knickers, and another ended his thoughtful report on wrestling in the local area with the words: 'seem like nice boys'.

You understand the problem. Cumberland and Westmorland Wrestling is a *tough sport*.

The costume, *sorry strip*, is an important element because it allows the judges to clearly see who hits the ground first. So when you're watching, don't snigger or you'll find yourself flying through the air with *your* undies on the outside... *if you're lucky*.

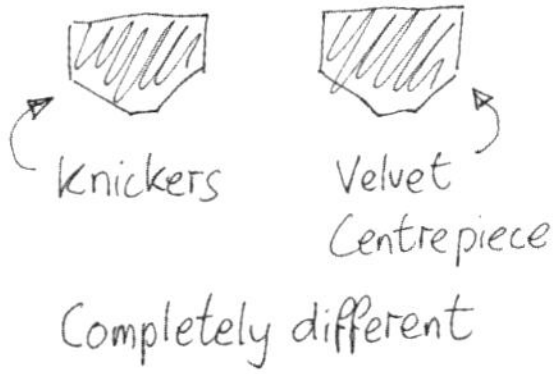

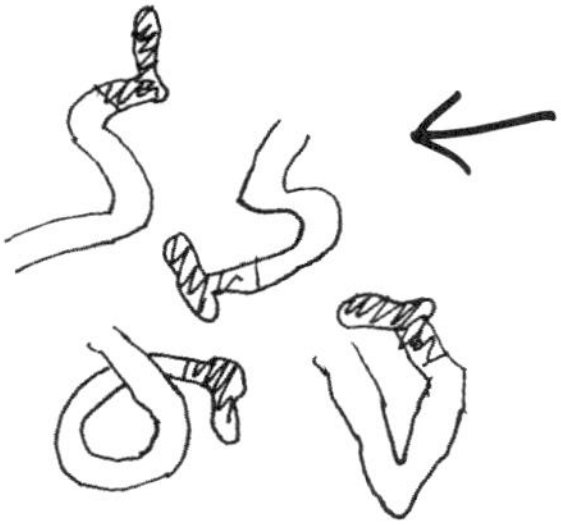

To get good at the sport your legs need to be able to do this:

Here are the rules: you grasp your opponent around the body with your chin on their right shoulder then use a series of *chips*, like an *outside stroke*, a *swinging hipe*, a *hank* or a straightforward *cross-buttock* to drop them without *brekkin' hod*. If it's a *dog-fall* you *tekk another hod*.

Simple as that.

CULTURAL CORNER #2

ART IN THE LAKES

The Lakes aren't all about slogging up mountains until your patellas grind into your tibias. We're a cultured bunch up here. Here's Melvyn, the Braggster, this time on a campsite near Wasdale...

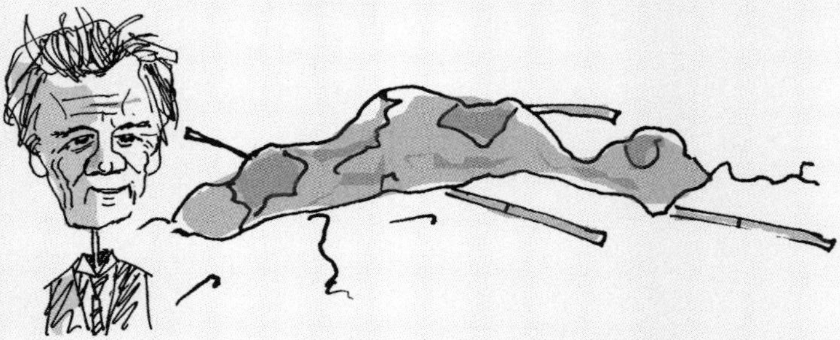

Over to you Melvyn:

"'Here I've found another magnificent piece of art. An affecting, or can I say heart-rending, perhaps harrowing image by Tracey Emin: 'The Unpitched Tent'.

"Words cannot explain how this visage of disconsolation and failure communicates the horrors of the modern world.

"Look at the way it has been thrown on the grass, abandoned by society, a despicable depiction of disappointment showing how.........................."

MEAL OUT

"The good lady wife took me out to a fancy restaurant last night to spend all my book royalties.

What a Scafell Pikin' outrage.

I couldn't understand a single thing from start to finish. Apparently I had a fricassee with al forno vegetables and a carpaccio side.

Wait, it gets worse. It was served on a roof tile!

The vegetables were foraged! Now I've been hungry many times out on those fells but I've rarely had to dig around in the undergrowth. Although the odd sheep dottel always filled a hole.

After that they gave me sorell with a compote bowl to go with the lardons on a charcuterie.

That was the last Esk Pikin' straw.

All I wanted, for God's sake, was some frutti di mare with pommes de terres and a bit of tomato coulis.

So that's exactly where I went afterwards."

SARAH NELSON

FIRST LADY OF GINGERBREAD

This is Sarah Nelson.

As you can see from her photo, Sarah had an infectious joyfulness that she let loose on the world in the form of gingerbread.

She had a tough life, so I will say no more about the photo.

She lived most of her days in poverty, she married a grave-digger with depression and her children all died of tuberculosis or cholera.

I feel bad now.

In 1850 she moved into Church Cottage in Grasmere, and after her husband and children died she turned to gingerbread. Not physically, but as a business.

People loved Sarah's gingerbread, and they still love it today. If you've not tried it, you should.

I like a happy ending so here's Sarah in one of her lighter moods. If Grasmere Gingerbread® wants this as their new sign I'm happy to discuss a price.

ESSENTIAL KNOWLEDGE

THE BEST TIME TO CAMP

Using my expert knowledge of the Lakes and my inhumanly poor weather predicting abilities, I'm going to tell you *the exact place and exact time* to camp in Cumbria to have an amazing experience.

Let's start with rain. Rain's difficult to avoid or predict, but solid facts have never been my thing, so here goes...

If you don't like the feeling of water cascading over your sleeping bag at 3am avoid the rainiest place in England – Seathwaite is out.

To be on the safe side we'll dispense with the whole of Borrowdale, no matter how gorgeous it is.

I'm being brutal.

On the fell tops there are gales around 100 days in every year. Thrashing around at the end of a guy rope is no fun, so we need to stay in the valleys.

May is the driest month, but let's call it least wet because there are still 12 rainy days on average. July is the warmest month with 12.9 rainy days. So let's choose June as a compromise. June 21st is too obvious and busy. Let's go crazy and opt for the 14th.

Now I don't know about you, but I don't like it too warm when camping because the inside of the tent gets unbearable as soon as the sun pops over the horizon. That's not a problem in the Lakes so completely disregard this paragraph.

Let's generalise further, if it's humanly possible.

According to knowledgeable weather people, the more you head inland towards Penrith the drier it gets.

So we're looking at Haweswater or Ullswater.

I love Haweswater, but the last time there was any civilisation down that wiggly road people from Manchester came along and submerged it under 84 billion litres of water.

That, and the fact there are no campsites, rules it out.

So we're left with Ullswater.

And I'm glad because Ullswater is my favourite lake, which is why I've skewed the results of this exhaustive study.

Pooley Bridge is out, because it's too busy with people who can't be bothered driving seven miles down the lake to get to the good scenery.

I think camping should be as wild as you can possibly get it. That's the point of it, otherwise you might as well pitch up in your garden until it gets cold then go inside to your electric blanket.

We're going down to the other end of Ullswater, between the lake and Place Fell, with a view stretching over majestic Helvellyn.

It's one of the most scenic places you can possibly imagine.

But where *exactly*?

Only one person can pause so massively over-long enough to build up the tension...

I'll leave you in the company of Dermot O'Leary...

Intentionally left blank to increase the stress beyond anything you can possibly stand...

Intentionally left blank to increase the perceived value of this book...

I'm really overdoing this now...

Couldn't be bothered drawing Dermot again.

See you at Side Farm on the 14th.

HUMPS & TUMPS

AW again:

"OK, I might as well tell you, there are other fell groups as well as mine. Not as good, obviously.

Now sit down, because this next bit is going to tickle your ribs.

In Scotland they have the Munros, named after Sir Hugh Munro, who compiled a list of all Scottish peaks with a summit over 3,000 feet back in 1891.

That's not the funny bit.

Alan Dawson in 1992 made another classification, for mountains that have a drop of 150 metres or more on all sides of the summit. He called them Marilyns!

Marilyns! See! Marilyns and Munros! Stop, my ribs!"

There are 55 Marilyns in the Lakes.

Then there are Anne and John Nuttall, who classified anything over 2,000 feet with a drop of 15 metres on either side as... let's think...

They called them the Nuttalls.

Alan Dawson can't stop naming hills. He also came up with the Hewitts (Hills in England, Wales and Ireland over 2,000 feet with a 30 metre drop), though I think he should have gone for The Dawsons.

Then Birkett created the Birketts – any Lakeland fell over 1,000 feet. You can also have:

→ Furths: Same as Munros but not in Scotland.

→ P600s (or 'majors'): Independent summits above 600 metres.

→ Humps: Drop of 100 metres on all sides.

→ Tumps: Hill separated from adjacent ones by 30 metres.

→ Bumps: Almost imperceptible incline that causes my children to cry.

ESSENTIAL KNOWLEDGE

THE ULTIMATE FELL FOR BIG HEADS

If you subscribe to the maximum results / minimum effort way of thinking and you want to climb just one hill, here's what I suggest:

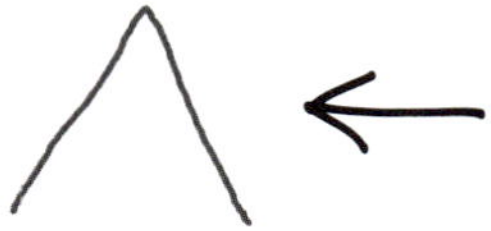

Just outside Keswick there's a great looking fell called Grisedale Pike. It looks a bit like this:

From Keswick it has the classic mountain shape, with a ridge all the way to the top.

There are some steep bits, but if you're going to brag you need to put a little effort in.

If you get to the top of this one fell then you get to take over as the most boring person in the universe.

LAKELAND STEREOTYPES #2

'PHOTOGRAPHER'

I'm here at Warnscale Bothy watching the dying embers of the sun as it dips below the summit of Mellbreak.

What a sensational sight this is going to be, captured in all its glory by me and my Fujifilm X-T30 with APS-C sensor and 8fps shooting rate.

Landscape photography is all about patience and technical excellence. You have to be prepared to go the extra mile to get that unique shot.

Individuality is the key, seeking out that classic view when the light is perfect and making it your own, giving it a fresh perspective that will capture the hearts of rich tourists on Keswick market.

The sun is melting...

It's time to get into position...

Say cheese Buttermere...

ACTUAL SURVIVAL SKILLS

A Survival Guide wouldn't be a Survival Guide without an actual survival skills section, so here it is:

→ 1. How to use a compass.

Twiddle the little plastic ring thing around a few times, look meaningfully north and place the compass on the map.

Then follow one of the many very wide Lake District paths back down the fell.

→ 2. How to source water.

Tilt your head back, open your mouth and wait.

3. How to find food.

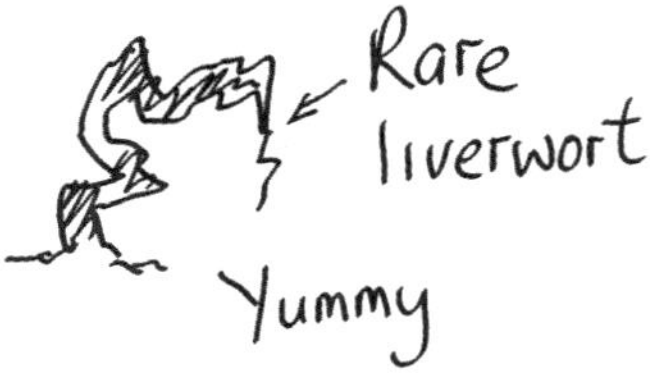

Find someone wearing a tall, white, round, pleated hat and pick what they're picking.

Chefs are always foraging.

4. Panic.

I've always found that running around waving your arms in the air doesn't help much, though it is a lot of fun. So this is optional.

5. Using a phone.

As a last resort phone your mam.

I get a better signal on the top of Scafell Pike than I do in my back garden.

ART IN THE LAKES

The Lakes aren't all about slogging up mountains until your patellas grind into your tibias. We're a cultured bunch up here. Here's Melvyn, the Braggster, this time on The South Bank...

Over to you Melvyn:

"Here we are on the South Bank (of Langstrath Beck) and down below us among the rocks in Blackmoss Pot is Henri Matisse's iconic 'Blue Nudes'.

"It's amazing to see them all together; they've only been seen like this a few times in the last 50 odd years, so this is a real thrill. I can't tell you how excited I am. This has really got me going. The way their bodies curve... thrown on the grass, abandoned by society, a despicable depiction of disappointment showing how............................"

...The Lakeland Winter Skinny Dipping Society were not happy.

SPEED DATING

'Hello, my name's Alfred, I'm a fellwanderer.'

'Pleased to...'

'Firstly, I won't have much time for you.'

'Well, it's not ideal ...'

'Can you drive?'

'Yes, I...'

'Would you want to accompany me on walks?'

'That sounds nice....'

'Would you speak to me during the walk?'

'Not if you don't...'

'Do I need to take my hat off at bedtime?'

'Not if you...'

'Get your rucksack.'

FARMERS & JAM

At some point while roaming the fells you may encounter a person in wellies riding a quad bike full of dogs.

This creature is called a *farmer*.

You never know what you're going to get with farmers. They're an unpredictable species.

To smooth the interaction, when speaking to them I recommend you speak in their language.

Start with *Arreet*.

Speak loudly, put your cheeks into it and string out the last bit of the word as long as you can. Like this:

With a friendly rapport struck up it's time for a weather conversation.

Approach the farmer carefully. If you can see a strange burning orangey ball in the sky try: *It's gey whaarm.*

If it looks like rain's coming then: *It's hossin it doon ower yonder.*

If it's cold and you've forgotten your hat:

Then a couple of compliments wouldn't go amiss.

If you see 15 sheep in a nearby field try this: *Champion bumfit yow int' fyeld.*

If the lane is nice: *Yer lonnin's barrie.*

If the farmer's still being miserable and you think he might originally be from Whitehaven (and you'll know because he'll look like this: ⟶ ⟶ ⟶ ⟶)

go for this: *Hoo jam eater*, thous a feckless divvey, a'll bray yer with me kebbie and hoy a styan inyer fyace.*

That should get a reaction, so *I'd lowp ower't yon gyat and leg it till yer paggered.*

* Just a quick note on the jam eating thing.

People from Workington on the west coast of Cumbria call people from Whitehaven, eight miles down the road, jam eaters, because back in the day they were so poor they couldn't afford meat in their sandwiches when they were down the pit.

To get back at the people from Workington, the jam eaters from Whitehaven thought long and hard and came up with a name to put down the people of Workington.

They called them jam eaters.

It's a very childish coast.

Here's a map to indicate where you might encounter a jam eater. The shaded area is a high risk zone. ⟶ ⟶ ⟶ ⟶

But it turns out that the real jam eaters are the cleverer ones because meat used to go off quickly in the humid atmosphere of the pits, whereas jam didn't, and that's why they ate it.

So who's the jam eater now?

You are.

FELL GREETINGS

Many of us go on the fells to get away from the hustle and bustle of life.

Nevertheless, when you're walking it's essential that you talk to your fellow walkers.

I'm not saying swap emails and get out your wedding photos. I am saying you should always acknowledge someone if you walk right past them.

Here are some guidelines for walking chit-chat:

Don't leave me hanging

When you meet a single walker, a simple nod, or a smile or a "ow-doo, my single hiking friend," is sufficient. Don't overdo it or they might press charges.

If the single hiker is a man in a flat cap wearing hiking gear made from wool I always give him an: "*Owz't ga'an,*" followed by "*It's fair hoyin it doon, eh?*" because I know he's a local and the chances are it'll be raining.

Be careful with this, because the phrase has to be said in a Cumbrian accent, not: "All right marrow, it's precipitating like billyo, don't you think," or it might sound like you're taking the wee out of him.

When you pass a hiking couple, I tend to opt for a more up-beat: "Hiya," followed by an appropriate weather-related comment:

Large groups are difficult, I prefer to say a loudish hello to the first person in the group and then smile and nod like a fool as I work my way down.

If there's a significant break in the group I have to repeat the process for the slowcoaches behind.

Alternatively, crowd surf.

If you're going uphill it's always good to add your favourite 'my legs are killing me' expression with some sort of 'phew' noise; it helps with bonding.

When passing kids if you're on the way down always say:

There's an ice-cream van at the top

When you meet at a viewpoint, choose one of these superlatives: 'amazing', 'marvellous' or 'stupendous', and gaze into the void with an enraptured expression.

Here's a series of expressions I recommend:

Don't be tempted to outstretch your arms in a 'I'm the king of the world' type of way. This only works in photos and looks silly when you're with others.

If someone is listening to their phone whilst walking, try this:

The important thing is to be friendly.

No one wants to hear a detailed narrative about how this walk compares to your ascent of the Eiger in 1957, but everyone likes a cheery hello and a smile.

So if you're one of those people who stare blankly ahead as you squeeze pass your fellow hiker on a narrow track, come on, stick to the guidelines outlined here.

One more thing...

If you meet someone wearing high heels or unlaced oversized baseball boots and jeans, forget everything I've said and completely blank them.

ESSENTIAL KNOWLEDGE

SURVIVING THE LAKE DISTRICT WITH CHILDREN #2

With the advent of mobile phones and goldfish attention spans you need to work a lot harder to keep your kids focussed on outdoor fun.

You need to plan *an adventure.*

The best kind of adventure for my kids involves cooking something bad for you and staying up late, which is why we were driving to the shores of Derwent Water at 8pm on Saturday night.

It was going to be a fun evening, I told them.

The kids strongly disagreed with me as we got out of the car and horizontal rain smacked into our faces.

(They're only young. Their love of rain hasn't matured yet.)

"It'll be fine when we get down to the lake," I said.

It wasn't.

We trudged down through the forest. 'Trudge' isn't a very positive word, but on this occasion it's the right one.

"It's easing off a little," I tried.

It wasn't.

At the shoreline I unfurled the secret bit of kit I haven't told you about yet. I threw my daughter's Quickpitch Tent (it's pink with unicorns on) into the wind. It popped up and our instant shelter blew down the shoreline.

This was the turning point.

Running after a tent is more fun than it sounds. The tent eventually got snagged in a tree in a sheltered bay. We sat in the door of the tent looking out onto the lake. There was wind, rain, mountains, waves, rustling trees... and us. No-one else. Just us.

Then an unexpected noise came from the tent. A noise I'd never heard outside in the rain before...

...The kids were laughing.

Mainly at the dog dragging sausages out of the rucksack. But at least they were laughing.

I wrestled the meat out of the dog's mouth and onto the stove. There's is nothing tastier in this whole world than pre-chewed sausages, cooked in the rain, on the shores of Derwent Water.

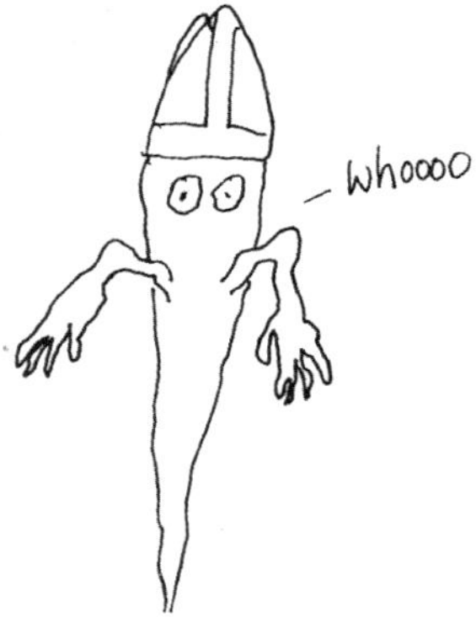

Soon it was dark. Now was the time to make up a story about the spectre of St Herbert, a hermit from St Herbert's Isle who to this day haunts the shadows of the lake shoreline looking for children eating sausages...

"Shut up, Dad, that's rubbish."

On the way back I pretended our head torches had broken and every skeletal branch was St Herbert's grasping hand.

By the time we got home it was nearly 11 o'clock.

As they were cleaning their teeth I asked them if they'd enjoyed themselves. "Ppfffgghhhhssshhh," they replied.

I waited until they'd finished cleaning their teeth and asked again.

"It was okay," they said.

You can expect no greater praise in the whole world from a couple of teenagers than "It was okay."

LAKELAND STEREOTYPES #3

'FELL RUNNER'

If you venture above the 1,000 feet level you will see this creature, I guarantee.

It can be identified by its red blotchy skin, its angular bone structure and, importantly, a little tube sticking out from its camel-like back.

The tube is some sort of life-support system, either for breathing or drinking, I'm not sure which.

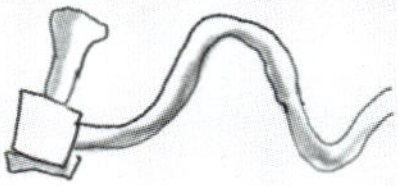

Its breath is raspy as it moves swiftly over the terrain.

Downhill you will hear the creaking and snapping of its specialised knee and ankle tendons.

It's not dangerous, but it can get grumpy if you don't get out of the way.

CUMBRIA'S GOT TALENT

We may not look like a talented bunch up here in the Northwest, but believe me, we're a lot more gifted than we look and definitely more gifted than those jokers in the Northeast.

"Divvent talk poo, like man."

"Awey with yer, gadgie, giz a bag o' crisps."

Shut up Ant and Dec. Answer me this:

Can yous two plough an acre of land in nine minutes and 49 seconds?

No, but Temple Sowerby farmer Joe Langcake can.

→ ...Which is World Record #1.

How long would it take you two losers to eat a Kit-Kat?

Cumbrian Daniel Dickinson can do it in 22.52 seconds.

“Whey, a’ll dee that easy, like.”

Without using his hands. → →

→ ...Which is World Record #2.

When you two chipmunks are showing eggs in an exhibition, how many times do you do it in a year? We can take both your scores for this one if you like.

“200, like.”

200 times, you say? Hard to believe, but if you say so.

Still not good enough though.

Because George Taylor showed his eggs off at 594 exhibitions *in a single year*.

→ ...World Record #3!

Do you have a stone skimming competition over there in the Northeast?

Can you stack pancakes to over a metre?

Do you have 300-year-old topiary in your gardens?

Have you seen 867 Supermen in one place?

→ ...World Records #4, 5, 6 and 7!

Here's Simon Cowell, his hand poised over the Golden Buzzer...

...He's just seen 1,080 people throwing shaving foam pies at each other in Ulverston...

→ ...World Record #8!

...We're through to the finals...

MOTIVATIONAL SPEAKER

'That Eric Robson made me do something hideous the other week.

It was supposed to motivate youngsters to get outdoors and off their phones.

I went to answer questions at an Outward Bound centre.

"Alfie, do you actually enjoy walking? Isn't it, like, hard work?"

That was the first question. They called me Alfie...! Even though they're younger than my newest pair of socks! Why would I want to encourage creatures like that onto the fells?

"Hey! Alf-myster, I have a virtual reality headset and can go anywhere I want. Why should I slog my guts out getting to the top of Scafell Pike?"

Because... you feel the air in your lungs, the breeze on your cheeks, the curlew's cry... And don't call me Alf-myster!

"Hey Alfie, the Alfster! Where can we buy a cap like yours?"

It was exactly then that this happened: →

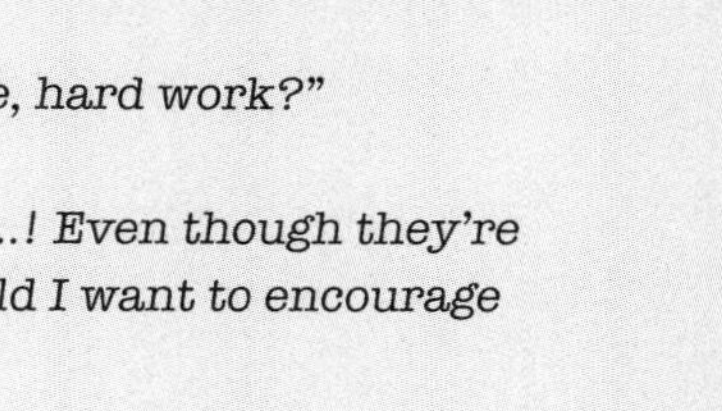

All the way to the top of Scafell Pike.'

COLERIDGE: HOUSE GUEST

Samuel Taylor Coleridge lived with the Wordsworths in Grasmere for 18 months. He was nursing a growing laudanum habit and no-one else wanted him. By all accounts he was a royal pain in the nethers.

"*Dorothy shut that blinkin' door, that dull sobbing draft, that moans and rakes upon the strings of this Aeolian lute, it's getting right on my nerves.*"

He insisted on taking cayenne pepper with his eggs, which he had to eat in a particular teacup.

"*Woman. Oh Dorothy, my genial spirits fail; should I gaze forever on this egg that lingers alone devoid of spicy capsicum? A grief without a pang, void, dark and drear and it tastes rubbish without it.*

"*My teacup! How can I lift the smothering weight from off my breast? My eyes bedimmed. And still I gaze – and with how blank an eye! I need my egg in my flippin' teacup with the cayenne pepper on top.*

"Bring me my teacup or I swear I will throw myself into the starless lake of blue.

"Finally woman, before I allow the viperous thoughts, that coil around my mind, to give you a bloody good telling off............"

EQUIPMENT REVIEW

TENT CARPET

Whatever you do, don't tell Ranulph Fiennes about this, but I have put together three justifications for owning a tent carpet.

→ **Justification #1:** In the mornings, when the tent is dripping with condensation and the ground is cold and covered in dew, you poke your toe out of the cosy inner tent trying to find your boot and your socks. Little do you know that one of the kids left your boot simmering on the BBQ last night and your socks have been eaten by the dog.

Your warm unprotected toe is going to have to touch down. *What would you rather have, Ranulph? The icy bite of a damp groundsheet or the velvety kiss of a soft tent carpet?*

One nil to me, I think.

→ **Justification #2:** You're outside your tent, the sun is shining and you're full of pasta. The kids are happily stealing tent pegs on the other side of the camp site. The world is amazing, or it would be if you could just have a nice lie down for an afternoon snooze. But, wait, the grass is still a bit damp and there are a couple of beetles scuttling about. How are you going to have your nap?

Not in this £9.99 camping chair that's for sure.

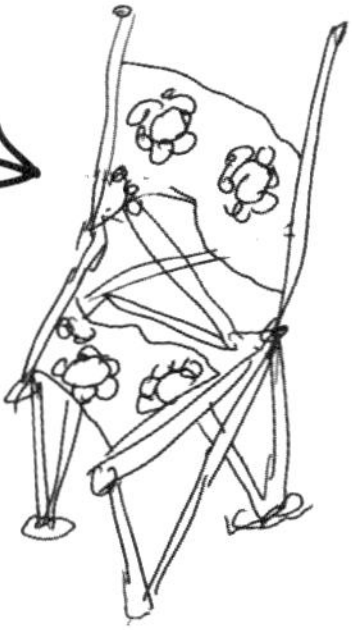

Don't worry. Reach inside your tent and slide out the tent carpet, plump it up so it catches the sun beaming down over Red Pike, then snuggle down and enjoy.

What do you have to say about that Ranulph?

→ **Justification #3:** You've made up some sarnies to eat on your evening walk. You've managed to get the kids to walk about a-mile-and-a-half, so well done for that, but now they are hungry and their legs have crumpled beneath them.

There's no picnic table or handy fallen tree. What do you sit on?

Then you remember that your tent carpet rolls up really small and you've packed it in the bottom of your rucksack. With one flick of your wrist the tent carpet unfurls into the world's biggest picnic mat.

Lay out your spread and tuck in.

← *Look how peeved Ranulph looks now.*

BEATRIX POTTER

If you walk down any street, lane or muddy path in the Lake District, Squirrel Nutkin has probably lost his tail there or the Flopsy Bunnies have been skinned alive by Mr McGregor just around the corner.

(I have chosen not to draw the skinned Flopsy Bunnies you'll be glad to know.)

Beatrix Potter first came to the Lakes on holiday in 1882.

Her parents rented Wray Castle.

Poor Beatrix. A castle. Pretty similar to what we rented on our last holiday.

From that moment, looking down on the mountains from the ramparts, Beatrix fell in love with the Lakes.

Everywhere you go has some Beatrix Potter connection.

She stayed at Lingholm (another dump) on the shores of Derwent Water. Here's a sketch. To give a sense of scale, the small square thing on the right represents my house.

Lingholm's vegetable garden inspired *Peter Rabbit*.

Owl Island in *Squirrel Nutkin* is really St Herbert's Isle in Derwent Water.

Little Town in Newlands Valley is where *The Tale of Mrs. Tiggy-Winkle* was set.

Fawe Park (yet another dump) has claimed *The Tale of Benjamin Bunny*.

After spending time near Keswick, Beatrix Potter moved to Hill Top in Near Sawrey and bought all the farms and land shown in the shaded area: → → →

Everywhere you go Peter Rabbit has been there first.

But Beatrix was a good sort.

On her death, she left all her property and prize Herdwicks to the National Trust so we can enjoy them to this day.

Inspired by this, I too will be leaving my most valuable possession to the National Trust.

You're welcome National Trust.

PUBLIC HEALTH ANNOUNCEMENT

Since this is a Survival Guide I thought I'd better mention a substance that is easily available throughout the Lake District.

Although the initial effects are quite pleasant there are DANGEROUS SIDE EFFECTS.

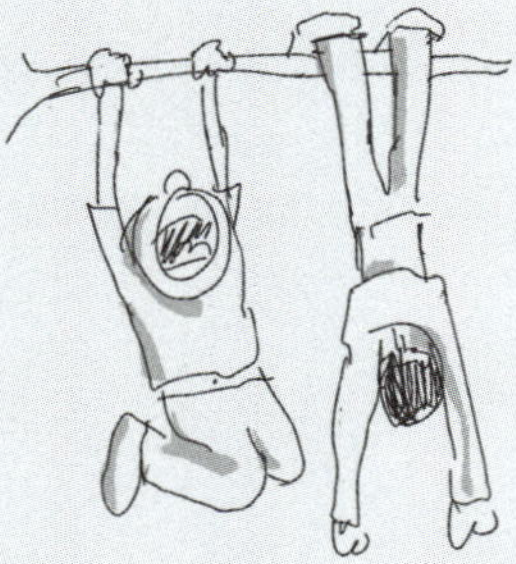

This is what happened within seven minutes of my kids getting some: →

The substance quickly passes through the small intestine and is absorbed into the bloodstream. It smashes into the pancreas, creating a ton of insulin which can only be released as explosive energy.

That's when you can't help but race for the nearest tree or vertical crag face and start climbing. You need to expend energy fast, so you start doing things you wouldn't normally do.

Many people have achieved too much under the influence of the substance, causing jealousy and bitterness among lazy people.

It is VERY, VERY DANGEROUS.

Kendal Mint Cake is sold at all ~~reputable~~... everywhere.

CUMBERLAND SAUSAGE

Whatever you do, don't mistake this:

For this:

No, I haven't been taking the dog for a walk.

This is a highly detailed illustration of the difference between the mighty Cumberland Sausage and any other sausage, which we in Cumbria call a 'normal sausage'.

'Normal' is said with a downturn of the features as if you've just stood in something nasty.

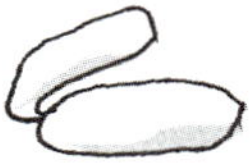

(That one *is* a dog poo, by the way, and as you can see it bears a very close resemblance to one of those normal sausages. Coincidence, I don't think.)

The Cumberland Sausage (note the double capitalisation as a mark of respect) is a single continuous coil. No pathetic links, just one solid spiral, sometimes up to four foot long.

It's pork and there's no mincing with this guy. It's just manly chunks of meat. Nor do we bother with herbs and spices; we just fire a load of pepper in there. Pork and pepper, *job done.*

Here's how to make it:

If you see 'Traditional Cumberland Sausage' on a menu it's been made in Cumbria and it'll be the best. Without the 'Traditional' at the front some thief has stolen and no doubt molested the recipe.

And if you ever see a Cumberland Sausage with links, not a continuous coil, take up your pitchfork and boot the kitchen door off its hinges.

Some things cannot be forgiven.

LAKELAND STEREOTYPES #4

'WAINWRIGHT OBSESSIVE'

The Wainwright Obsessive always starts a conversation with the most obscure crag or ghyll reference they can think of.

"It's pretty rough coming up Tarn Whithup Sike these days, so I tend to descend via Brazzelhazel Crag instead, or, for variety, by way of sheepfold and mine workings (disused)."

The Obsessive's ability to read a map is an attempt to impress and intimidate you.

Stay calm.

It's only preamble before they get into the meat of the conversation.

"Trying to bag six today, which will take me up to 1,070, since I've done them all five times already.

"I find people who've only done the Wainwrights four times nauseating. Do you..?"

"Totally."

Now is the section of the conversation where you will hear random fell names plus a Sharp Edge and Lord's Rake thrown in.

Bide your time... It's coming...

When you hear this: "And the time I went up Jack's Rake..."

Go: *"Jack's Rake, oh yes, that reminds me a bit of the three-day expedition I did up the North Spur of the Aiguille du Chardonnet in Chamonix..."*

If you can manage the slightest French accent when pronouncing the place name, even better.

"...The exposure on the rocky granite climb to Eperon Migot was..."

They should be gone by now.

ESSENTIAL KNOWLEDGE

WHY AUTUMN'S THE BEST SEASON

If you're planning a trip to the Lakes, come in autumn.
Here are five reasons why:

→ **1. Trees**

You know how the Americans go on about New England in the Fall and how the colours change and how *freakin' awesome* it all is.

Well, it's not as good as the Lake District.

Period.

→ **2. Pub fires**

In autumn pub fires start to get lit. I subconsciously plan my walks to accidentally end at one of my favourite pubs. *Clever, eh?*

My wife usually skips the walk and meets me there.

Even cleverer, eh?

→ **3. Tingliness**

I don't know about you but I get a tingly feeling when I think I'm the only person on the mountain.

A steady rainfall on the hood of your jacket as you trek up a remote gorge is a cosy feeling isn't it? I haven't a clue how to draw 'tingliness' so I've just squiggled some lines. Doesn't quite capture the moment...

I tend to walk on my own a bit more in autumn. I thought it was because my friends, wife and kids were fair-weather walkers. Now I'm thinking all this talk of tingliness is putting people off.

4. Mars Bars

Mars Bars reach their optimum temperature in autumn. Throw a bar in your bag, walk up a fell and by the time you get to the top it will have reached prime crunchiness. A firm clunk as you bite into the chocolate coating is what dreams are made of.

5. Crispy leaves

This is more for my dog than me. A forest full of autumnal, crispy leaves blowing around is Doggy Disney to my dog. Every leaf that whizzes past her nostrils or scutters up the path in front of her is like the first leaf she's ever seen that can do that.

You may rightly say that Mars Bars and crispy leaves can be found anywhere. They can. But the leaves are crispier here and the Mars Bars more crunchy.

SURVIVAL ESSENTIALS

WILD CAMPING ETIQUETTE

You know when a total stranger pitches a tent in your garden without permission, in full view of your patio doors, then starts a fire on your lawn, stuffs a few empty beer cans into your rockery and leaves it all for you to tidy up the next day?

That's what it feels like when I see a load of tents camped by Styhead Tarn in the middle of the afternoon.

Wild campers

Now I know wild campers are wild and don't like rules etc., but here are a few easy ones to follow:

→ **Try and keep out of my garden.**

→ **Be discrete.**
If there's nowhere else, at least keep off the patio.
And no I'm not making you a cup of tea.

→ **Only wild camp above 450 metres.**
Which is roughly three miles up the road from mine towards Caldbeck.

→ **If you need a poo,** which you will after a Wayfarer meal, ask next door. Or bury it a foot deep (two feet if it's a curry).

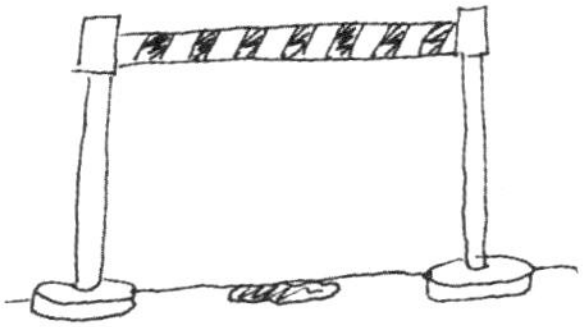

→ **Stay one night and move on.**
Which is what I say to all my guests.

To summarise: keep out of the way, clean up and watch where you poo.

Advice you'll have heard a million times from your mum.

CULTURAL CORNER #4

PHILOSOPHY IN THE LAKES

The Lakes aren't all about slogging up mountains until your patellas grind into your tibias. We're a cultured bunch up here. Here's Melvyn in WIgton's Hare & Hounds...

Over to you Melvyn:

"Here I am discussing very clever things with a fellow Cumbrian:

"So Cumbrian, I believe the Norwegian philosopher Petre Zessel Wapffe's essay 'The Last Defender' encapsulates the concept of existentialism in a slightly more salubrious way than Nietzsche's seminal doodioflips."

"Exactly, my friend; Epicureanism, the precursor to the aforementioned existentialism, I totally agree."

"Absolutely, when you're sentient and judicious, thinking about a time when you cease to proliferate and be cognisant is pointless."

"Your choice to savour your paltry existence, my random acquaintance, without the necessity for meaning is pure genius."

Life sorted

HOW TO GET BATTERED

If you fancy getting a punch in the face, here's what to do:

Point out to locals that the best place to put a wind turbine is in a windy place, for example, the top of Helvellyn or, even better, Windy Gap.

Admittedly you don't want every ridge and mountain to be full of turbines.

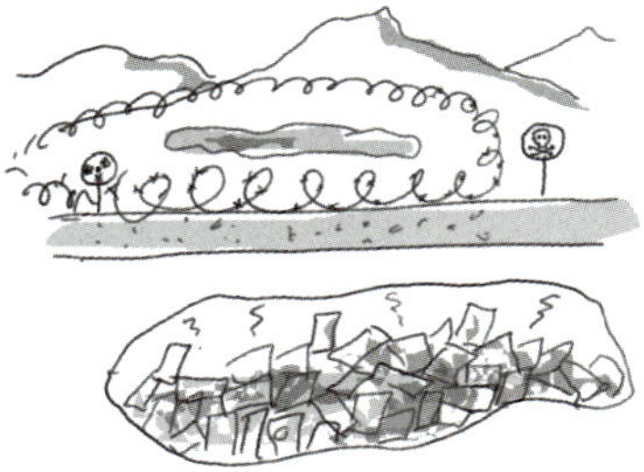

That's why we need nuclear energy. And where better to store the waste than out of the way under our tarns?

Making large areas of the National Park restricted access will also cut down on fell erosion.

(If that's actually a thing. I've climbed Scafell Pike loads of times and it always seems the same size to me. Look:)

Don't forget to say how hard work it is walking up Scafell Pike, and that what's needed is a zip-wire all the way from the top leading down to a McDonalds on the shores of Wast Water.

How good would that be?

And if you have a second home, don't forget to mention how affordable it was compared to your Surrey mansion and how it's left empty for most of the year anyway.

If you get to the end of this list of topics, you're not in Cumbria.

TACKLING HARDKNOTT PASS

If you want to drive Hardknott Pass this is the type of vehicle you require:

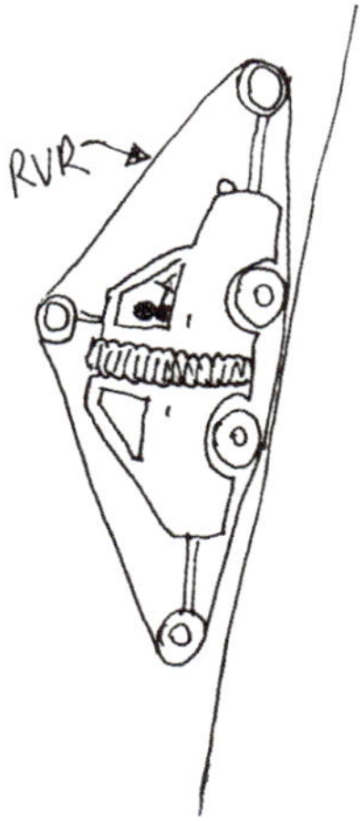

It has a flexible central area for the tight turns and an RVR (Rolling Velcro Road) system for extra grip.

Engineers out there may ask what's keeping the RVR on the road, if the Velcro revolves around the car but there's no opposing Velcro on the road.

It's a good question. (Please view my detailed Autocad drawings at www.get-a-grip.co.uk.)

CHOICE

THE CHOICE

Every day in the Lake District there is a choice to be made.

It's a simple choice, but nevertheless a choice. Just like my choice to use choice too many times on this page.

Here it is.

You wake up and you can either do this:

Or you can do this:

It's your choice.

ESSENTIAL KNOWLEDGE

THE HISTORY OF CUMBRIA

If surviving the Lakes in the present day without this Guide is tough, imagine what it was like 400 years ago.

Basically, if you weren't keen on having your house burnt down every six months, Cumbria wouldn't have been your first choice.

Sure, you'd be able to snap up a great, dual aspect, south-facing country retreat with bags of outside space overlooking a lake for next to nothing.

But you'd have regular cold callers.

And cold callers in those days weren't trying to get you to swap electricity providers.

Instead they turned up on horses with pikes and blazing torches, and the deal was they got everything you owned and the pike wasn't stuck into you or, alternatively, they got everything you owned and the pike *was* stuck into you.

It was a simple and very persuasive offer, much less complicated than all these different energy tariffs we have to remember now.

Let's see what lessons we can learn 1,000 years ago from King Dunmail.

KING DUNMAIL

Around AD950 Dunmail wasn't just a shopping centre between Workington and Flimby, he was the King of Cumbria and Cumbria stretched all the way to Glasgow.

I haven't a clue what Dunmail looked like but I'm going to give him a Sean Bean-look from *Game of Thrones* because he's hard and northern.

King Edmund I, who was grandson of Alfred the Great and probably wanted a 'Great' after his name as well, decided to do something with his life so he moved in on Cumbria. He teamed up with Malcolm I of Scotland and sadly defeated Dunmail between Grasmere and Thirlmere.

Edmund gave all of Cumbria to Malcolm.

Legend has it that Edmund himself killed Dunmail and then poked Dunmail's sons' eyes out for good measure.

The captured Cumbrians were ordered to collect rocks and pile them on top of King Dunmail's body, forming a cairn that is still there today on Dunmail Raise. Now for the good bit: other Cumbrians escaped with Dunmail's crown, climbed up to Grisedale Tarn and threw the crown in to keep it safe until Dunmail would come again to lead them.

Every year the ghostly warriors are said to return to the tarn, recover the crown then carry it down to the cairn on Dunmail Raise. There they strike the cairn with their spears and a voice is heard from deep inside the stones, saying:

...Which is all very well, but not when your fighters are rapidly decomposing.

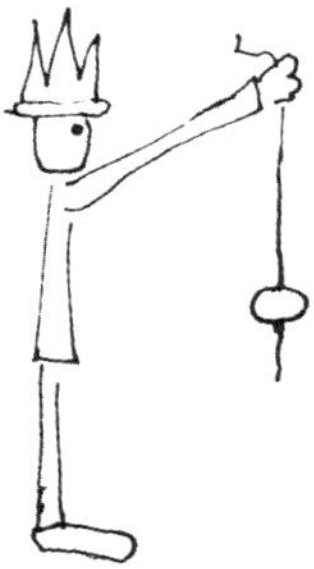

From that moment onwards, Cumbria became the Wild West.

William II – how come dads always get better names? – wanted to do some conquering of his own

William captured Carlisle for England, then King David I of Scotland got it back, then Edward I wound up the whole of Scotland with some kerfuffle about the successor to the Scottish throne.

William Wallace and Robert the Bruce got involved and the whole of Cumbria was a battle ground for the next 300 years.

(That's William Wallace by the way, not George Michael.)

With all this cross-border killing and plundering going on, what's the worst thing you can think of doing? Killing yourself?

The inhabitants of the Borderlands decided to do just that.

THE BORDER REIVERS

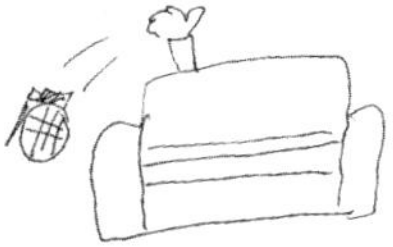

Question: What happens when you leave the kids to their own devices?

Answer: They start attacking each other and stealing each other's things.

Not my kids, obviously, but it can happen.

Without any structure Cumbria kicked off.

Large families from north and south of the shifting border divided their land equally among various children, clans formed and these clans were even more childish and vicious than my... I mean, someone else's kids.

They became known as the Border Reivers. Hobbies included looting, stealing livestock and kicking cats for no reason.

But their favourite thing by far was kicking the cats of other clans.

They didn't care about England or Scotland or which King was which; all they cared about was fighting for their clan.

They enjoyed it so much they kept at it for 400 years.

The mayhem went on until 1603 when James VI of Scotland became James I of England and the country was united.

The Reiver clans were hunted down and killed.

But that's not the end of it. In 1642 the English Civil War broke out and Cumbria sided with the King. Scottish Parliamentarians weren't happy and hammered Carlisle with cannons for eight months.

It was then retaken by Royalists and taken back by Parliament. By which time Carlisle looked like this: →

So what's the lesson here?

...which is advice you can take with you whichever county you visit.

WILLIAM WORDSWORTH

Today there are not many poets, not even Jay-Z or Kanye, who can change the perceptions of a whole nation.

Wordsworth did.

Before Wordsworth moved to the Lake District, the fells of Cumbria were scary.

In the early 18th century, Daniel Defoe shuddered in his curly wig as he passed the mountains in his carriage. He called them disgusting and wondered how any civilised person would want to live here.

"Shut yer face, Defoe, or I'll shove that curly wig... no, I mean, don't be preposterous Daniel, we are all civilised up here. Why don't you ask William, he seems to like it?"

Wordsworth *did* like it.

He spent his childhood in Cockermouth, then when his parents died he moved to Penrith. After a while in inferior places around the world William moved to Grasmere to escape the 'hell for eyes and ears' that he called London.

He took up residence in Dove Cottage, and started writing the best poetry of his life.

In the process he implanted the Lakeland landscape into the consciousness of a nation.

The visitors came. Then Wordsworth turned grumpy for the remainder of his life.

SURVIVAL ESSENTIALS

UNITED UTILITIES SAVES THE WORLD

With climate change impacting on the planet both in Lakeland and overseas, here's a map showing how United Utilities plans to extend its pipelines to save the world from drought over the coming decades:

MISCELLANY

FUTURE OF THE LAKE DISTRICT

It's okay, they've gone

MARGARET LUGNER'S GARDEN

Margaret Lugner lived in a small cottage near Eskdale Green.

She grew delphiniums, mostly *Blue Lace* and *Yalanci*, and had a garden that covered the land from Sunny Brow all the way to Gelwyddog Farm.

It was huge.

Her land looked a bit like this, if delphiniums looked like someone had just squiggled a pen a round for five minutes:

As you know, butterflies love delphiniums.

In the summer they swoop down the River Esk in their millions. They have done this for thousands of years and it's a wonderful sight if you time it right. Margaret's garden is where they're heading.

Even before Margaret cultivated her garden, delphiniums grew there. It's a site that's been recognised by the World Wildlife Federation since 1973.

When they land in her garden, it's like the garden's a living creature.

It looks a bit like this, if squiggling a pen around and then getting bored and putting it into Photoshop is like a load of butterflies:

Margaret was in her garden in June 1987 when the butterflies started to get *wahahee*, which is a scientific term that roughly translates as 'extreme agitation'.

Butterflies rarely get *wahahee*. In fact scientists have only witnessed the behaviour twice in the past 40 years.

During a *wahahee* the butterflies pick a single object to *menteur*, which is the butterfly version of swarming or hovering. Butterflies might choose to *menteur* a tree, a rock, sometimes even a house. But on this occasion it was Mrs Lugner.

A million butterflies descended on poor Margaret. Witnesses, having a couple of beers across the road at the Charlatan Hotel, saw what they thought was a huge mass of insects rising into the air.

Then they saw legs sticking out of the bottom, kicking and twisting.

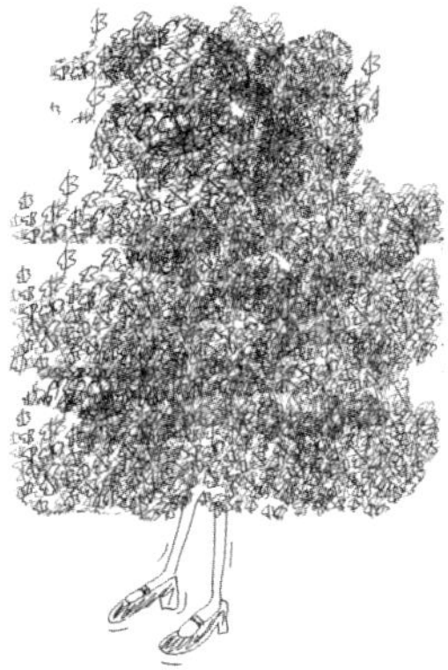

Now, I wouldn't be drawing silly sketches of Margaret if this didn't turn out okay, so don't panic.

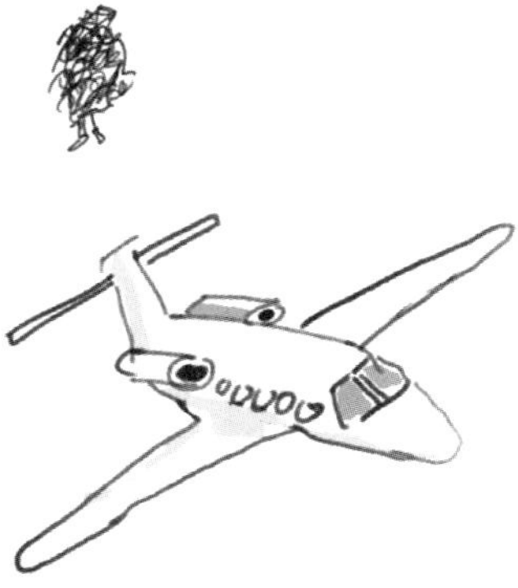

Margaret was lifted into the air by the mass of butterflies and carried down the valley towards Shammer Tarn.

Witnesses said she reached about 300 feet in the air.

As you can imagine it must have been a terrifying experience.

Margaret was carried along the valley and to the left of Irton Pike.

It was only when she reached the pub at Santon Bridge that the butterflies ran out of steam and she landed at the Bridge Inn garden right next to Will Ritson's cow sheds that have been carved out of turnips...

...Which was a bit of a coincidence, because the Bridge Inn is the location of the World's Biggest Liar Competition that takes place every year in memory of one of Wasdale's most famous sons.

But this strange story of Mrs Lugner *is definitely all true.*

DAYS OUT

GO APE

Before you even think about taking the kids to Go Ape in Whinlatter or Grizedale Forest, here are a couple of stretches I recommend you do in preparation:

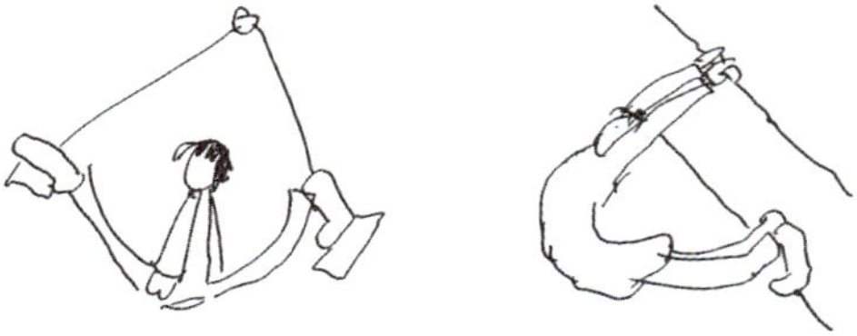

Next, go down to your local football pitch and do this for a while each day:

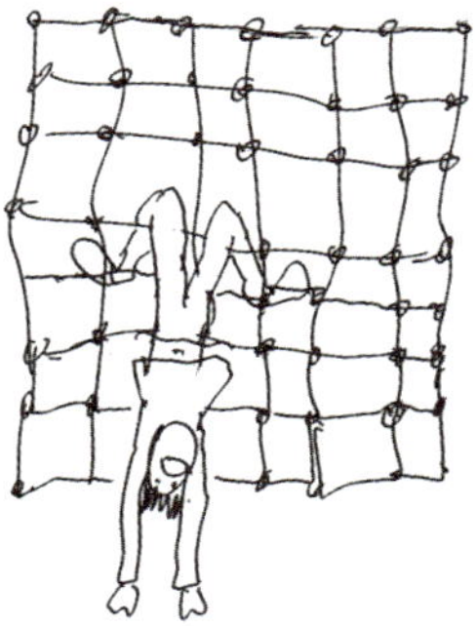

These exercises are designed to rupture your *pubic symphysis*, your *rhomboidius major* and your *posterior cruciate ligment* so you have a really good excuse not to go.

LAKELAND STEREOTYPES #5

'MOTOR HOMER'

Take a close look at this: → → →

It's a good-natured creature, which doesn't want to do anyone any harm. All it wants to do is move slowly through the countryside.

← ← Take a close look at this:

Inside is a good-natured creature, which doesn't want to do anyone any harm. All it wants to do is move slowly through the countryside.

The only difference between these two creatures is the tortoise sits in a box in your conservatory and the other doesn't.

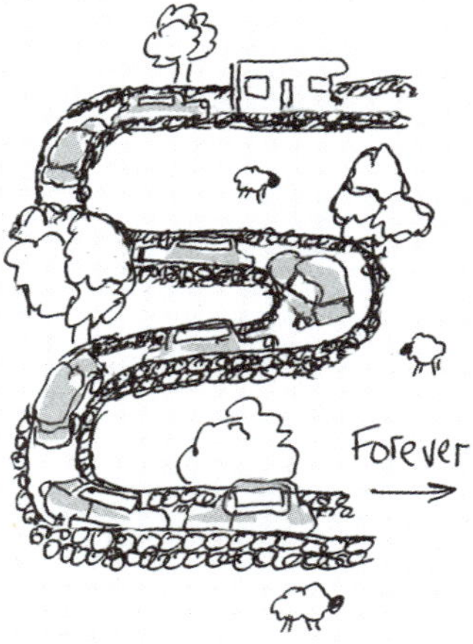

PUB CRAWL

Before I start, there are a lot of other Lake District pubs that I like, and could easily add to this list, but I don't want you to think I have a problem.

Here is a pub crawl that involves the 555 bus, starting at Windermere and finishing in, well who cares, but let's say Keswick.

In order to get this section accurate I felt the need to do some hands-on research, so I phoned a couple of alcoholics I've known for years and set off.

We started in Windermere.

→ 1. The Crafty Baa, Windermere

The Crafty Baa is small and quirky and it has won awards. The AA voted it Pub of the Year 2018/19 and I agree with them. The decor is 80% recycled, but the beer – they assure me – is not.

The Crafty Pale Ale is tasty. The only problem is you get the beer in a *schooner*.

Not one of these, which would be cool: → → →

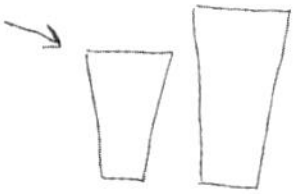

← ← ← But one of these.

We had two thirds of a pint and then jumped on the 555 at St Mary's Church, back on the A591.

→ 2. The Golden Rule, Ambleside

Get off the bus just as you're leaving Ambleside, near the main car park and tiny house that's a bridge. If your beer gut will allow it, walk back up Smithy Brow, the steep incline across the road.

Now this might be an age thing, but The Golden Rule is perfect; no music, no food, just several rooms to drink in and talk rubbish.

Getting back to the bus is all downhill, which is where the night will be heading if that's how stimulating the *craic* is.

→ 3. Badger Bar, Rydal

Get off the bus in the centre of Rydal, if you can find a centre.

There is the option of visiting Rydal Mount, yet another home of Wordsworth, instead of going to the pub.

Be aware that taking this option may hurt.

(Went a bit *Batman* there, sorry.)

In Badger Bar you might start tripping up and knocking into things and spilling drink. This has nothing to do with the beer. It's because Badger Bar's floor is a bit skewwhiff, with chunks of rock sticking up and tables that could do with a beer mat shoving under a leg.

Be careful. If you do trip your mates will assume you're a lightweight.

Next stop Grasmere.

→ 4. Tweedies Bar, Grasmere

I seem to finish a lot of walks in or around Grasmere and then my boots take over and against my will I am dragged into Tweedies Bar.

Tweedies Bar is five minutes' walk from the bus stop down Langdale Road.

It's got stone floors, solid tables and stinky hikers – and that's what I like.

The barman told us we could "spend time exploring his extensive range of beers," so that's what we did.

As with every great journey of exploration, there are moments of pure joy when you're with the bestest friends that ever existed, ever.

"You've always been there for me, man."

And then there are tougher times.

"What, Man City? No, no, no. Man City are rubbish pal and so are you."

But we got through it and were soon back on the bus.

Did you know the back seat has perfect acoustics?

→ 5. The King's Head Inn, Thirlmere

I was going to recommend The King's Head, at the other end of Thirlmere after the lake disappears to the left, but it was far too posh for us idiots, so we kept rolling on into Keswick.

Keswick is the end of the line for the 555, so unfortunately 'You'll Never Walk Alone' was cut short before we could go into falsetto for the big finish. What a shame.

In Keswick we may have gone into a couple of other pubs, The Golden Lion, The Oddfellows...

...But I definitely remember the Dog & Gun.

6. Dog & Gun, Keswick

No matter what hour of the day you go into this pub it's always busy.

We tucked into a few Keswick Brewery Beers and the Dog & Gun's famous beer-absorbing Hungarian goulash.

I love the Log & Bun, it's my favourite. But I also love the what's-its-name, The Georgy, the Georgy Porgey, you can eat a cow there, and... other stuff... and... brink more deer...

...The stupid doors... I mean, floors... are wonky there too...

It's at this moment I decide to go home.

But I'd had too many beers, so I didn't.

THE PROFESSOR OF ADVENTURE

Forget Bear Grylls, leaping over rocks with a tube sticking out of his bum to collect life-saving moisture from the bladder of a dead duck-billed platypus.

Move over Ben Fogle and his week in the wilderness, just off the A66, talking softly with an accountant who got bored with maths.

If you want to know about adventure, there's only one person you need to know about.

The Man himself...

The Professor of Adventure...

The Caveman of Borrowdale...

The...

(I'm not good at this.)

It's MILLICAN DALTON. → → →

In his early 30s Millican packed in a boring office job in London and headed off into the wilderness.

Borrowdale to be more precise.

Every summer for almost 50 years Millican lived in a cave on the side of Castle Crag.

He climbed and he smoke, he smoked and he climbed. It was a simple life, breathing in the fresh Lakeland air filtered through a Woodbine.

He made money as a guide and climber and had the freedom of never, ever using Sure for Men or Jasmin and Ylang-Ylang soap.

Hey Millican, wave goodbye.

EGREMONT CRAB FAIR

If you're walking through the market town of Egremont and someone pulls you into the market hall and throws a horse's collar over your head it's not a compliment.

Someone has spotted your potential and you've been entered into the Egremont Crab Fair World Gurning Competition.

The event has happened every year since 1267.

700 years of gurning and Charles Darwin's theories on natural selection have taken their toll on the community. This can clearly be seen on a quick walk down the main street.

I'm from Workington, further up the coast, where we've had the 'Good God, You're Incredibly Handsome' competition for 10,000 years and, yet again, Charles Darwin's theory has been proven.

MELV & ALF'S BOOK REVIEW

OUTRO

MY FELL WALKING MISTAKES

As we're coming to the end of this Guide, it's time for me to come clean on some of my fell walking mistakes.

This could be a whole book, so I'll précis viciously.

One of my problems is I love to mistake dry streams for paths until I'm stuck in a deep ghyll.

Also sheep trods confuse me and I find peat hags enjoyable to fall into.

Sorry to the couple eating their breakfast in the long grass on top of Loadpot Hill. It was early, there wasn't a soul around, so I had a wee enjoying the scenery.

When complete, I looked down and saw them 10 yards in front of me, nestled in the undergrowth, not enjoying the scenery.

Sorry, too, to the mountain biker who came over a ridge near Dale Head and saw something even more unpleasant.

In a storm on Crinkle Crags I put my rucksack in a 'safe place' and never saw it again.

I overestimated my bravery on the slimy rocks of Cust's Gully.

A stag chased me over Brock Crags.

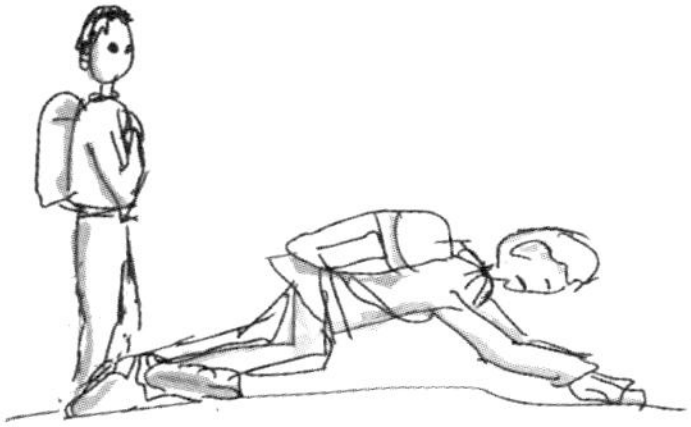

I crawled for a mile on my hands and knees on top of Skiddaw in 80mph winds. (I don't actually know the wind speed but didn't think I would get away with 100mph.)

I also need to apologise to the guy who was so thrilled to have finally scaled Scafell Pike. It had been one of his dreams for years after a major operation. I didn't have the heart to tell him he'd taken a left at Esk Hause and was actually on Esk Pike...

...Sorry, my friend, you never made it.

Please don't look behind you

OUTRO

THE HEARTFELT ENDING

That's it, you've survived.

I remember my first time at the top of a fell. It was a moment of magic, a revelation so unexpected that I stood transfixed, unable to believe my eyes. I saw mountain ranges, one after another, the nearer starkly etched, those beyond fading into the blue distance. God was in his heaven that day...

Okay, sorry Alfred, I just wanted something inspirational to finish.

THE REAL ENDING

I've lived in the Lakes for most of my life and have survived. It's not that difficult, especially now you've reached the end of this Guide.

The mountains are mostly friendly. No matter what Daniel Defoe said.

If you wake early, don't lie around in bed; this is when the magic happens.

Get onto Striding Edge at 5am with the sun rising behind you over Ullswater. Then you can do this... → → →

...without looking an absolute idiot.

What d'you say Melv?

Yes, yes... couldn't agree more.

Beware butterflies going into *wahahee* and remember most Cumbrian's are complete and utter liars.

But their hearts are in the right place. → →

Watch out for mythical creatures wandering the fells.

Alfie, the Alf-myster (I'm sure he would've been fine with me calling him that) is part of Lakeland.

AW's books aren't just books, they're mini adventures, to be read, and more importantly, lived in the very steps that he took.

My days walking with Wainwright have been some of the best of my life, second only to boring people about them in the Dog & Gun.

If you're taking children onto the fells and you follow the rules outlined in the Guide this won't happen:

(That's me by the way, when the Haribos have run out and we're five miles from home.)

Finally, don't mention zip-wires, wind turbines or nuclear waste; velvet centrepieces aren't undies; Sarah Nelson is fun; no-one knows who the jam eater is; and pub floors are wonky. Honest.

Enjoy your time in the Lakes. Saving your life has been my pleasure.

OUTRO

FINAL ASSESSMENT

Before you go off into the Cumbrian countryside I need to know you've been paying attention and you're going to be safe. Only proceed if you get all these questions right:

1. Firstly, 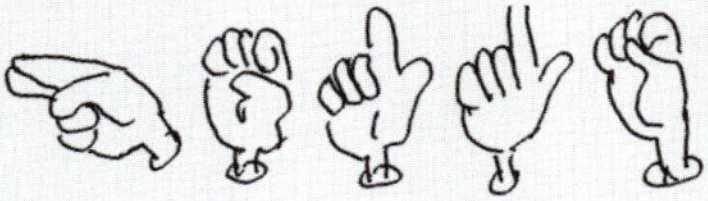

2. Multiple choice. What is this guy saying (page 13)? →

a. I don't care.
b. Still don't care.
c. Kill me now.

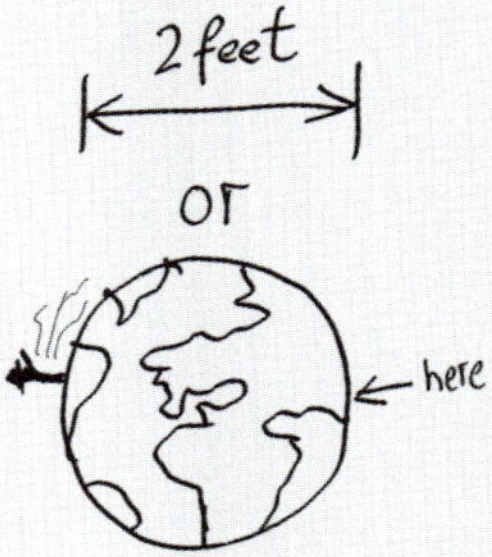

3. What is the recommended safe distance from Millican Dalton's armpit (page 112)?

4. What is the most interesting mountain in the Lakes (page 29)?

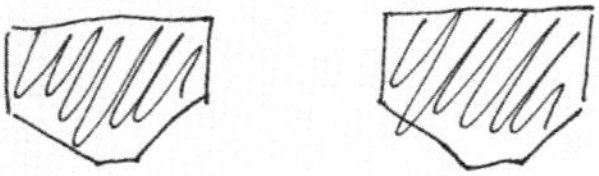

5. Spot the difference between the knickers and the velvet centrepiece – there are 386 in all (page 32).

6. Is it possible to do this without shame (page 58)?

7. How many times does the word 'Wainwright' appear in this book? When you have the answer go to the Dog & Gun in Keswick and meet up with the guy from Question 2. You'll get on great.

8. Which mountains are nicer?

a. The Lake District ones

b. or all the other horrible ones?

Congratulations adventurer. You may now venture forth into our great county in the knowledge that you'll most likely survive the trip.

Well done.

THE LAKE DISTRICT SURVIVAL GUIDE

Written and illustrated by Ian Young © 2019.
Photo of Sarah Nelson © Grasmere Gingerbread®.
Designed by Chapman Design.
Edited by David Felton.

Printed on woodland-friendly FSC stock.

ISBN 978-1-9998940-5-4

A catalogue for this book is available from the British Library.

Published October 2019 by Jake Island Ltd,
3 Brunt How, Loughrigg, Cumbria LA22 9HE.

The Lake District Survival Guide is an Inspired by Lakeland title.

For news and other publications see inspiredbylakeland.co.uk
To get in touch email hello@inspiredbylakeland.co.uk

If you like Ian's drawings, his merchandise can be found at
skwiggles.co.uk

INSPIRED BY LAKELAND

FSC www.fsc.org MIX Paper from responsible sources FSC® C014138